DISCIPLINE:
A Shared
Experience

v

ACKNOWLEDGEMENTS

Many people contributed to the publication of this book. We wish especially to thank Dr. Richard H. Usher, Dr. Fred Richards and Dr. Anne C. Richards for their reading and editing of the manuscript through several revisions. Also, we express our appreciation to Mr. Ted Shields whose encouragement and suggestions exceeded what one might ordinarily expect from a publisher. Finally, our thanks and appreciation to Mrs. Sheri Campbell for her typing of the manuscript.

Library of Congress Number: 73-76694
International Standard Book Number: 0-88310-011-8

DEDICATION

To my wife, Marie, and my son, David, who share the experience of life with me.

I.D.W.

To my mother and father, f, f, and s.

W.M.S.

TABLE OF CONTENTS

INTRODUCTION

Discipline, in its most effective form, is a shared experience. Too often, however, it can become a sort of psychological tug of war between teachers and students. The classroom becomes a battleground on which teachers seek to subdue and coerce students into doing things the teachers think are important and students don't. Rather than a shared, mutually enhancing experience, discipline becomes a clash of wills.

As a consequence of the battleground approach to discipline, our schools have very often become grim and sometimes inhumane places. Recently, it was reported that the second largest school district in the nation voted to continue "spanking" in its schools. Another news release reported that a school board in New Mexico decreed that *rubber hoses* could *no longer* be used as instruments of corporal punishment; instead, all schools were ordered to use *leather straps*! Extreme examples? We would hope so but at this writing there are not five states in the United States that actively discourage teachers from hitting students. Many even encourage it. Regretfully, they are examples portraying a system in which students and teachers perceive one another as enemies, as objects to be dominated and subdued or as obstacles to be removed.

The use of corporal punishment is totally absent from this book; it is our belief that hitting or physically abusing children in the name of establishing order or enforcing discipline is, at best, naive. It is an act of ignorance. In light of what psychologists now know about fostering human growth and mental health, it is as obsolete and inexcusable as flogging sailors at sea to keep order on a ship.

We believe that children learn discipline when it is personally meaningful to them and shared with concerned and significant others. Children do not learn to make decisions by having decisions made for them; nor do they learn responsibility by being denied responsibility. Responsibility and self control are learned best when the opportunity to assume responsibility is readily available and when this opportunity is shared and experienced with others.

It is true that students, like adults, do not always make the right decisions and as a consequence make mistakes. Aware of and accepting this, one mistake the teacher can avoid making is seeing the teacher's role as one of assuming all authority and responsibility in the classroom. The role of the adult, when discipline is viewed as a shared and learned experience, is to act as an experienced guide and exemplar of ways to best achieve cooperation, order, excitement and community in the classroom. Sharing this role with the students, the teacher aids them in creating a classroom in which assuming responsibility and acquiring discipline become a natural part of the cirriculum.

The situations presented in this book are situations that might occur anywhere in the school from preschool to junior high school. Often it is an attitude toward discipline we are trying to convey and not specific answers to problems - although the text offers prescriptive suggestions. The responses appropriate for a pre-schooler may not be appropriate for a junior high school student. Therefore, they should not be taken literally but as suggestions for creating trust and sharing responsibility in the classroom. The "do's" are guidelines, not hard and fast rules. They are meant to help you move toward a philosophy of discipline as a meaningful and shared experience for both students and teachers. If the book has done this, it will have served its purpose well. This is our wish.

I.D.W.
W.M.S.
Greeley, Colorado

**Responding
to the
Negative**

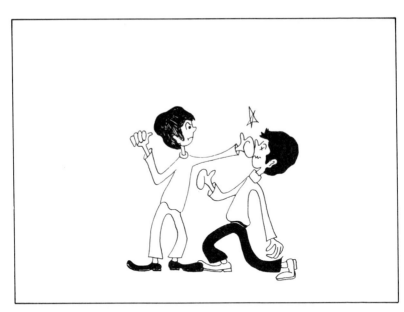

FIGHTING

DON'T Do Nothing

2

DO

Something To Stop It

Fighting is a crisis situation. You have to do something to stop the fight. The thing you do might be wrong but often we don't have time to stop and think of the best solution. Do something. Later, if you made a mistake, you can apologize.

HITTING

DON'T Hit Him

"Mike, since you hit Carol, I'm going to hit you."

DO

Stop Him and Accept His Feelings

"Mike, sometimes I feel like hitting too. But . . . people are not for hitting."

Often we are the models for the things we tell children not to do. Hitting is an example. If we tell children not to hit and try to make them stop by hitting them, we tell them, in effect, that hitting is exactly the thing to do. One thing to try is to establish a place in the classroom where hitting is legitimate - a hitting place. Tell students, "When you are angry, frustrated or want to hit something, go to the hitting place" (a punching bag, cushion or anything that can be hit hard is all that is needed).

WETTING PANTS

DON'T Make It a Big Deal

"Ron, don't you know better than that?!"

DO

Treat It Naturally

"Oh, gosh, sometimes that happens. Run, clean up."

We have to face the fact that there is no way to save the child embarrassment in this situation. All we can do is try to treat the situation as naturally as we can and try to prevent embarrassment from becoming humiliation. After the child has gone to clean up you might go to see if you can help.

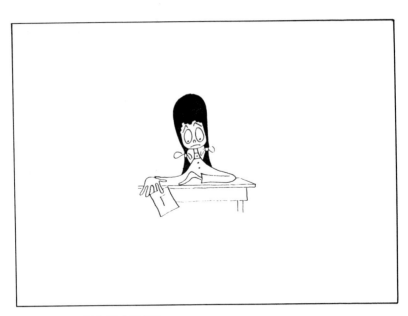

FAILURE

DON'T Use It as a Weapon

"Gwen, if you get another F, you'll flunk."

8

DO

Take Pressure Off the Child

"Gwen, sometimes people don't understand my questions. Let's talk about them."

There are many reasons a child can fail a test. 1) The questions are vague, 2) the questions are too difficult or 3) the child didn't study, might be among them. Whatever the reason, the teacher's job is to encourage learning - not to fail people or merely grade or sort them. In order to accomplish this the teacher may have to regive the test, create a different kind of test and encourage the child for the next tests. Why not give tests which fail no one or put tests aside for awhile and dialogue about issues and concerns with the subject matter?

BREAKING (BY ACCIDENT)

DON'T Punish the Child

"Kim, go to the office!"

DO

Offer Help

"Whoops! Let's clean this up."

There is no need to punish children for mistakes. They already feel guilty when they are clumsy. There is no need to make them feel worse.

BREAKING (ON PURPOSE)

DON'T Ignore It

DO

Explore His Feelings

"Ray, you must really be angry."

There is no need to ask why the child did what he did. It is more important to let him talk about it. It is more important to provide an opportunity for his anger and frustration to come out than it is to actively punish the child. Let him take care of the broken object (he may have to pay for it) and talk about a better way to express anger. Do not deny his feelings of anger. They are real. Perhaps, together, you can discover ways of expressing anger that don't hurt other people or their property.

RUNNING AWAY

"I'm Leaving!"

DON'T Be Sarcastic

"Can I help you pack your bag?"

DO

Ask a Question
& Express Your Own Feelings

"You must really be having a terrible time here today? What can we do to have a better time? I'll feel a lot better when I know you're enjoying yourself."

Asking a question provides an opening for dialogue. When the child begins to answer we can gain clues about why he is running away and what we can do to help him or take the pressure off him.

CRYING

DON'T Humiliate

"Keith, big boys don't cry. If you want to sound like a little girl you can cry."

16

DO

Get the Child Alone

If the child wants to cry, let him cry. If he wants to explain later why he was crying, let him. Crying can result from a lot of things. Some might be: 1) hitting - then comfort him, 2) falling down - examine the hurt or 3) mystery - let him cry and talk later if he wants.

RACISM
"That's awfully white of you."

DON'T Ignore It

DO

Seize the Opportunity

"Shirley, what do you mean when you say that?"

Whenever anyone makes a statement that smacks of racism, especially children, there is an opportunity to talk about one of the pressing problems of our day. Children in school need to explore the ideas of racism, prejudice and intolerance. Teacher-initiated discussion might begin by saying, "The other day I heard a statement . . . Have you ever heard anyone say that?" If we create opportunities for children to explore their own feelings about people different from themselves then we create the opportunity for a society not as plagued by intolerance as ours.

DISOBEYING SCHOOL RULES (DRESS CODE)

DON'T Send the child home or to the Principal

"Larry, I want you to go to the Principal's office."

DO

Tell the Truth

"Larry, I can't let you wear your shirt like that because it's against a school rule."

This is a situation that occurs every now and then at schools because, for some reason, schools have seen it necessary to legislate student fashion. Actually, there is no need for the teacher to involve personal standards of dress at all. Instead of talking about dress talk about the rule. This need not be a moral stance but it can be a practical one. Ignoring such things can cause one to lose a job needlessly and senselessly. If the children want to know the reason behind the school rule then it is a good opportunity for the children to learn about social action. Have them form a committee to see the Principal for an explanation and action. In this way, you can be truthful and provide the opportunity for the students to take action on their own.

GRAFFITI

DON'T Discourage It

"Fool's names and fool's faces always appear in public places."

DO

Encourage It

"I've made a special graffiti board and if you want to write anything on it, Steve, do. It's fun!"

We are forever trying to get children to express themselves. Yet, we sometimes pass up the fun ways of expression. Build a graffiti board and let the children use it. It is a good means of expression. It can also provide a good source of information on the atmosphere of the class. You may use it yourself. (See Marking on Walls).

PRACTICAL JOKE

DON'T Deny Your Feelings

DO

Respond

If it hurts, yell. Take a joke in good humor if you can. If you can't take it in good humor, respond with whatever feelings you have - anger, frustration or fear. Probably anything is appropriate - yelling, lecturing or crying. Do it all and then forget about it. It is not a crime to be human in a classroom. It is not a crime to express your own human feelings. When children play tricks on teachers it doesn't always mean they dislike them. Sometimes it may mean they like them. Don't jump to any conclusions. Don't demand a public confession.

WRITING IN BOOKS

DON'T Demand a Fine

"Kathy, you're going to have to pay 10¢ for every page you wrote on."

DO

Ignore It

Underlining meaningful sentences or phrases or writing notes in margins should be viewed as constructive use of books rather than misuse. Too often schools purchase expensive materials and equipment only to isolate them from educational purposes. There is a distinction between use and abuse. Intentional distruction such as tearing out pages or cutting up pages should be dealt with firmly (see Breaking - on purpose). Remember equipment is meant to be used; don't elevate "wear and tear" over learning.

HURT (REALLY)

DON'T Tell Him Not to Cry

"Max, don't cry. You're O.K. and crying won't help."

DO

Tend His Wounds and Comfort Him

"Let's take care of that."

If a child is really hurt, help him and don't humiliate him by telling him he shouldn't cry. Tend to his hurt.

The important thing is to be able to tell the difference between a hurt and a non-hurt.

HURT (NOT REALLY)

DON'T Get Excited

"Oh, Peter, are you hurt!?"

DO

Describe the Act

"Whoops, you fell down!"

Children fall down all the time and they are not really hurt unless some agitated adult thinks they should be. By describing the act you can find out whether the child is really hurt or not and at the same time not communicate your fear to the child.

THE PHANTOM

DON'T Demand a Public Confession

"All right, class, I want to know right now who wrote this on the board."

DO

The Unexpected

If people are not able to predict your acts, it returns the dynamics of the classroom to you. Often, doing the unexpected makes a classroom a lively, joyful place where children want to be - it can help establish rapport. Perhaps, it takes a teacher with a sense of humor.

THROWING THINGS

DON'T Use Scare Tactics

"Donna, you know you shouldn't throw pencils. You could put out someone's eye!"

DO

Return the Object to Its Owner

"Here's your pencil, Donna. Next time hand it to Kathy. Don't throw it."

This is a private matter between you and the student. The student is doing something you don't want her to do. There is no need to call the student to the attention of the entire class. Return the pencil and state clearly what behavior you expect. You do not have to lecture. Treat the interaction as a natural thing without malice or judgment.

BACK TALK
"Why do we have to do this sissy math?"

DON'T Make It a Confrontation

"Don't you talk back to me!"

DO

Explore Feelings

"I can see you have strong feelings about Math."

If a child is talking back to an adult, she must have something invested in the situation. Breaking the child's will, pride or dignity is excessive cruelty in the short run and ineffective in the long run. Ask yourself, "What sort of pressure did I put on her?" "How can I take it off?" Instead of getting into a fight with words, get into a discussion of feelings.

COMING IN LATE

DON'T Criticize

"Steve, you're late to class. Can't you get here on time?"

DO

Welcome Him

"Hi! Nice to see you."

There is no reason to criticize the child. Be happy he's there.

(If such behavior persists you might check to see if there is a problem at home or in school. If there is, discuss it privately.)

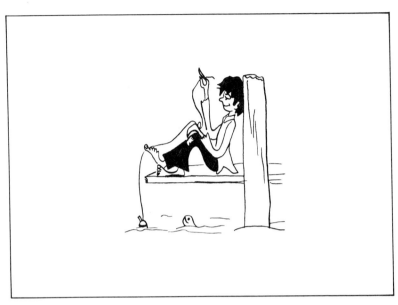

TRUANCY

DON'T Interrogate the Child

"Bruce, what are you doing out here fishing?"

DO

Demonstrate Concern

"Bruce, we missed you at school. Evan brought his pet cobra, it was something!"

School should not be a place to be feared. If children are welcomed back to school without malice then school can become a friendly place. School can become a place that does not have to be avoided.

RUDENESS TO OTHER
CHILDREN - INTERRUPTING

Girl: "The capital of Colorado is . . . Boy: "Denver!!"

DON'T Model the Bad Habit

Teacher interrupting boy, "Wes, don't interrupt."

DO

Ignore It

Let the children handle it themselves. It is a part of social learning.

RUDENESS TO ADULTS - INTERRUPTING

Teacher: "Today we are going to . . ."
Girl: "Teacher, can I change the calendar?"

DON'T Model the Bad Habit

Girl: "Teacher, can I . . ."
Teacher: "Brenda, don't interrupt."

DO

Model a Good Habit

Girl: *Teacher, can I change the calendar?"*
Teacher: *is quiet, then, "It irritates me to be interrupted."*

This is a teaching situation. Wait until the child is finished
and then say something about it. Don't interrupt. Describe
how it makes you feel rather than lecturing the child on
manners.

45

TATTLING
"Kathy stole the ball."

DON'T Keep It Confidential

"Kathy, someone told me you stole the ball."

DO

Bring It Out in the Open

"Dale, are you willing to tell me that in front of Kathy?"

A person has the right to be faced by his accusers. If the accuser is not willing to face the person, nothing should be done about it.

TEASING (FRIENDLY)

DON'T Ask Why

"Mike, why did you pull Wendy's hair?"

DO

Intervene with a Substitute Act

"Mike, will you go get the reading books for me?"

In a situation like this we must decide whether or not it is really disturbing anyone. If it is, then we interrupt the situation somehow. If it isn't bothering anyone, ignore it. It is probably not wise to ask a little boy why he is pulling a little girl's hair. It may be because he likes her and any self-respecting little boy is not going to admit that! You would probably force him into a lie. Don't ask is better advice.

TEASING (MALICIOUS)
"Look at that crippled kid. He walks like a duck in mud."

DON'T Ignore It

DO

Have a Town Meeting

"Stop everything."

Stop everything in class because this is a senseless and cruel common occurrence. Sit down and have a meeting in which the entire class participates in a discussion of people's feelings and how important they are. It is not necessary for the teacher to do much more than to suggest the topic and act as a "traffic director". Let the children discuss the issues with your guidance.

CLASSROOM BUZZ

DON'T Read Them the Riot Act

"If you keep this up, you'll be the last class to go to lunch."

DO

Get Their Attention

"Hey!"

Sometimes it is just necessary to get everyone's attention at once. The "do" here assumes you have done all the courteous things - "May I have your attention" and so forth. If that is so, yell, whistle, shout, ring a bell, clap your hands or make a loud noise any way you can. Then say what you have to say without malice and continue the class. Don't give a lecture.

SPEECH DEFECT - STUTTERING
"Th-th-the ca-ca-capital of Ne-ne-nebraska is Li-li-lincoln."

DON'T Try to Correct It
"Linda, slow down next time and you won't have so much trouble."

DO

Seek Professional Help

Stuttering is not always a permanent speech problem. But in later stages it can become a very difficult problem with which to work. Find a speech specialist. Often, without proper training, our good intentions can do more to hinder than to help. Also, let this stand as an example for any special problems with which you do not feel qualified to deal.

MESSY WORK

DON'T Put the Kid Down

"Steve, this is a terrible paper. Many words are misspelled, the English is terrible and the paper itself is a mess."

DO

Decide What's Important

"I had to overlook the messiness but I'm glad I did. Your idea of trust is really exciting."

What is most important? Is it that the paper is messy? Is it a good paper? Is it the first paper? If it is a good student who ordinarily turns in excellent work, the paper might signal some drastic change in the life of the student. If it is, then it is a signal he wants to talk to someone. If it is the first paper a student has ever turned in, then it is a signal of the child's viewing the school in a new light. It would be foolish to reject a child's first tentative efforts to do school work. You have to decide what is most important and act on your hunch. If it doesn't pan out, then you try another hunch.

LOOKING UP DRESS

DON'T Scold

"Danny, it's not nice to look up girls' dresses. Don't do it any more."

DO

Think About It

Think about it to decide if it is a passing event. If it is, ignore it. If it is exploration in a natural way, try to satisfy his curiosity and the curiosity of the entire class with discussions. If you believe it represents an over-concern with sex, then seek professional advice and help.

DRAWING "DIRTY" PICTURES

DON'T Make it Public

"Look what Ray is doing!"

DO

Put Your Hands on Child's Shoulders

The child is not particularly disturbing anyone if he is drawing at his desk, he is just not paying attention to the class. You need some way to bring him back to the class. You do not need to pass judgment on him. You don't have to say anything; he knows why you are there. He will probably just put the drawing away and begin to pay attention.

DEPRESSED OR WITHDRAWN

DON'T Ignore It

DO

Talk to the Child

"Coleen, would you like some help with your math?"

When a child is depressed or withdrawn, giving attention might help. You don't need to ask what's wrong; at least, not right away. If the child wants to talk about it and you give her the chance, she will.

POOR HYGIENE

DON'T Humiliate the Child

"Mike, don't you ever take a bath? I don't want you to come in smelling like that again."

DO

Have a Unit on Hygiene

Telling a child that he smells bad in front of the class is a hurtful thing. It would be better not to say anything about it to him. Get toothbrushes, combs, wash cloths and a towel for each student. Each morning then, the first class would be hygiene in which every student would be involved in the study and practice of cleanliness. If it involves clothes, you might visit the parents.

NEGATIVE FEELINGS
"I hate Mr. Grudge!"

DON'T Deny the Child's Feelings
"Steve, you shouldn't talk that way about your teacher. He's a wonderful man."

DO

Talk with the Child

"Steve, I can see you're really upset. Do you want to talk about it?"

Let the child express his feelings. In fact, there is nothing wrong with the feeling of hating someone. Feelings are all legitimate. We must not make people ashamed of what they feel. Often it is the repressed feelings that culminate in an unacceptable behavior. All of us have feelings. It is the job of adults to help children explore their feelings so they can learn how to deal effectively with them. Accept the child's feelings in the same way you hope your feelings will be accepted.

DISOBEDIENCE

DON'T Make Writing a Punishment

"Bonnie, I want you to write 'I will obey my teacher' 100 times."

DO

Discuss It

"Bonnie, I think we're having a problem. Let's talk about it."

Don't ever use writing as a punishment for anything. If you do, writing will never be enjoyable and the child will associate writing with punishment. It is not the job of a teacher to teach children to dislike school or school work. If a child is disobedient, then talk with the child about it but do not assign extra work as punishment.

POTTY MOUTH
"I don't want to do this shitty assignment!"

DON'T Ignore Him

DO

Give the Child Attention

"Wes, let's come up with something you do want to do."

When a child uses profanity, pay attention to the child not to the child's language. Yelling and scolding him will not solve the problem. In fact, it reinforces the language. Very often children use "dirty" words for their power. The violation is really more aesthetic than moral. Thus, by ignoring the language you take away its power and consequently its use. This does not mean you ignore the child. If a child needs attention - give it to him. Denying attention to children who need it only contributes to their problem behavior and they may resort to more and more bizarre behavior to get attention.

CHEATING

DON'T Rip It Up
"Kim, I am going to rip this up and you're going to get a zero on it."

DO

Talk About It

"Kim, we both know you cheated on the test. It must be very important to you."

Before you do anything rash, think about the reasons the child cheated. You may not have explained the rules as clearly as you thought you had. The child may be under unbearable pressure. In any case, you are not a judge but a teacher. Your job is to teach; to promote learning. If you can teach a value such as not cheating, do it. But do not humiliate and demean the child in the process. Decide on a mutually agreeable solution.

RUNNING AROUND

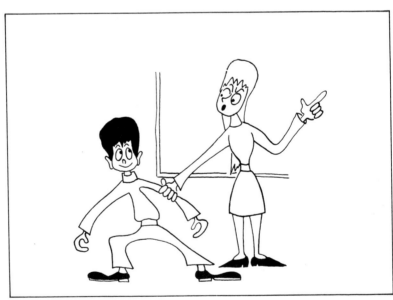

DON'T Threaten the Child
"Larry, if you don't sit down and be quiet, I'm going to send you to the principal."

DO

Get the Child to Do Something

"Larry, would you please hand out the books for spelling and write the new words on the board?"

When a child is running around disturbing the class, divert his attention and energy into something that helps you. Also arrange a suitable environment so the child can get rid of his excess energy throughout the day. Arrange a legitimate place to run around and make noise. Always being quiet is probably not even an easy thing for adults.

MARKING ON WALLS

DON'T Simply Scold the Child
"Now, Carol, you know better than to do that. I want you to go sit in your seat and stay there."

DO

Give Appropriate Attention

"Carol, I want you to clean up the wall."

When the child writes on a wall or does some other destructive act, the child must be held responsible for it. If she breaks a window, she should pay for it (with money, not pride or dignity). Letting a child get by with a misdeed or asking someone else to clean up the child's mess will not teach the child respect for others or others' property.

STEALING

DON'T Ask for a Confession

"I found these scissors in someone's desk. Do you want to tell me anything, Roy?"

DO

Discuss It

"Roy, we both know you took the scissors. Now, where do we go from here? What should we do about it?

Never ask for a public confession if you already know who did something. Confront the child with the evidence you have, tell him you know he did it and then take it from there. If you ask in front of the entire class you will humiliate the child. You may also force the child to lie in an attempt to save face in front of the class and create an unnecessary confrontation. In any case, we all have the right to be confronted with the evidence against us. Trying to trick the child into a confession serves no useful purpose.

TALKING

DON'T Yell

"Brad and Tony! If I hear you two again I'll . . .

DO

Discuss Your Feelings

"When you talk in class, it upsets me. What can we do about it?"

This will be a common situation. Usually the whole class will not be interrupted but when it is, you have to do something about it. Making threats doesn't work. The best approach seems to be enlisting the help of the people who are disturbing you and the class.

Pay Attention
to the
Good Things

SENSITIVITY

"I saw a pretty flower."

DON'T Deny the child's feelings by ignoring them

DO

Respond to the sensitivity

"That's nice, Brenda, tell me about it."

Don't stifle sensitivity by thoughtlessness. Even if you feel a little pushed, take the time to respond to a child's feelings. Pay attention to the good things.

HELPING TEACHER

DON'T Make a Big Thing of It

"Look, Roger watered my plants."

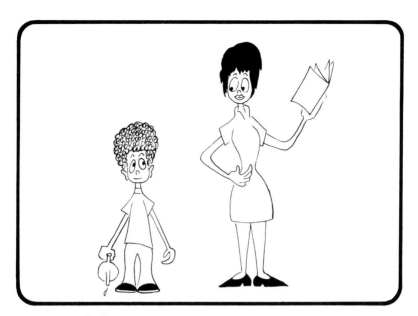

DO

Treat It Naturally
"Thank you, Roger, that's nice of you."

Helpfulness is something you really want to encourage so it is important to treat it as if it were almost expected but still appreciated. Pay attention to the good things.

HELPING OTHERS
"Let me help you with your boots."

DON'T Make It Public
"Craig is helping Donna with her boots. Why can't some of you others be that helpful?"

DO

Respond Privately

"Craig, I saw you helping Donna with her boots. I know Donna was very grateful. Thank you."

You must use your own judgment here. If a little boy is helping a little girl, he may feel embarrassed if you talk about it. But sometimes it is good to respond openly to helpfulness. However, it is wrong to use the helpfulness of one child as a weapon to use against the other children. It sets the child up as an adversary to his classmates. Again, this is a judgment on your part. Pay attention to the good things.

CARING

DON'T Discourage It

"Bobby, get back in your seat."

DO

Respond to the Behavior

"I can see he is."

This is the kind of behavior we want to encourage. You can do this by showing the child that his act of caring is good and noticed. Pay attention to the good things.

SHARING

"Here, Margie, you can have half of my sandwich since you forgot your lunch."

DON'T Be Crabby

"Margie, you can just sit there since you forgot your lunch. Jane shouldn't have to give up her lunch just because you're so forgetful."

DO

Show Your Approval

"It's very nice when people share."

It is important here to remember that you need not embarrass the child who forgot her lunch while approving of the child who shared. You want to insure the possibility that the day you forget your lunch the children will share! Pay attention to the good things.

SYMPATHIZING
"I guess old people must really be lonely."

DON'T Be Callous
"When you think about it, they're no worse off than anybody else."

DO

Encourage the Action

"What do you think we could do about it?"

It is important not to let an opportunity to turn sympathy into action slip by. This can become an opportunity to allow children and the aged to teach and learn from each other. Pay attention to the good things.

COOPERATION

DON'T Ignore It

DO

Compliment Them on It

"This group is really doing a great job together."

In complimenting a group on their cooperation you do two things at once: 1) you compliment them on their work and 2) on their cooperation. Pay attention to the good things.

GOOD STUDENT

DON'T Compare Him with Others

"Fred, you're the best student in class."

DO

Encourage Him
"You really seem to enjoy learning new things"

If a child is bright, it is important to encourage him - not only his work but his self-concept as well. Do the same thing with children who are not as bright and teaching becomes the great profession you dreamed it could be! Pay attention to the good things.,

HARD WORKER

DON'T Neglect Her

DO

Compliment and Assist Her

"I can see you're really working hard, Anne. Can I help you?"

Children who work hard are demonstrating a positive value.
Here, too, you should challenge and encourage the child.
This is the kind of child you can count on when you want
something done. Pay attention to the good things.

CREATIVITY

DON'T Be Pompous

"This story isn't very realistic."

DO

Encourage It

"This is really an unusual paper, Jeannie. I've never seen the word 'wallpole' used for a monster's name."

You have to teach yourself to recognize the many ways children are creative. Some may be creative writers or speakers. Other children may be creative artists. Encourage creativity in whatever form it occurs. Pay attention to the good things.

The Do's
and Don't's
of Discipline

Don't

1. Don't give children a choice unless you are willing to accept their decision.

2. Don't deny a child's feelings.

3. Don't demand respect.

4. Don't demand a behavior you can't or don't intend to enforce.

5. Don't try to buy a child's affection.

6. Don't be afraid to make mistakes.

7. Don't always expect children to tell you why they did something.

8. Don't demand a confession of guilt.

9. Don't teach children to be responsible by taking responsibility away from them.

10. Don't expect children to behave like adults.

Do

1. Do accept choices if you give them.

2. Do accept feelings.

3. Do earn respect.

4. Do enforce the rules you set.

5. Do earn affection.

6. Do act when it is necessary and think about it later.

7. Do realize there are reasons why children can't express why or won't express why they did something.

8. Do respect the 5th and 6th amendments to the Constitution for children.

9. Do give children responsibility. If you do give them a job and they fail, don't take it away from them. Give them a second chance.

10. Do learn what is reasonable to expect from a child.

Reprinted by permission of Dr. Richard H Usher; University of Northern Colorado; Greeley, Colorado.

It's Done!

DATE DUE